Wher
Machu Picchu?

by Megan Stine

illustrated by John O'Brien

Penguin Workshop

For Sara, Max, and Milton—MS

For Linda—JOB

PENGUIN WORKSHOP
An imprint of Penguin Random House LLC, New York

First published in the United States of America by Penguin Workshop, an imprint of
Penguin Random House LLC, New York, 2018

Visit us online at penguinrandomhouse.com.

Library of Congress Control Number: 2017047141

Printed in the United States of America

ISBN 9780515159615   10 9 8 7

Contents

Where Is Machu Picchu?

Flocks of green parrots flew overhead in the jungle. The air was sticky and damp. It was July 24, 1911. Hiram Bingham and six other explorers had been trekking through the jungles of South America for days. The thirty-five-year-old professor from Yale University was on a quest. He was searching for the place where an ancient people called the Incas had once lived and then died out four hundred years before.

Ever since childhood, Hiram had dreamed of a life of adventure. Now he was finally living it. He was leading an expedition that included a doctor, a naturalist, and a geographer. They were in Peru, where Hiram hoped to discover the ruins of the lost Inca city of Vilcabamba. He wanted to become famous.

The beauty of the jungle was breathtaking. Orchids bloomed everywhere. Snowcapped mountains towered above. Hiram and his fellow explorers followed a path along a river. They passed waterfalls and tree-size ferns.

Hiram later wrote, "I know of no place in the world which can compare with it."

But after five days, some in the group were tired. They didn't want to keep going. The journey had been hard. They were riding mules through a jungle that was overgrown with vines and buzzing with insects. Poisonous snakes slithered about. They decided to stay behind at the camp to wash their clothes or hunt for butterflies.

So on the sixth morning of the trek, Hiram set out with just one other companion—a sergeant from the Peruvian government. They were led by a local guide named Melchor Arteaga. Melchor had said that if they crossed the river and climbed two thousand feet up the mountain, they would find some ruins—ancient buildings that had fallen apart.

Could this be the magnificent city Hiram Bingham was looking for?

Hiram sort of doubted it. He had a rule for himself: Whenever someone told him fabulous stories of lost treasure, Hiram reminded himself that it might be just a story.

Still, he was curious. He was also determined and energetic. So he followed Melchor across a shaky bridge over rushing water. The bridge was made of only a few logs tied with vines. Melchor and the sergeant walked across the wobbly bridge, but Hiram felt safer crawling on his hands and knees. Then he followed the guide up a steep trail for more than an hour, part of the way on all fours.

By the time they reached the ridge of the mountain, Hiram and the sergeant were exhausted. And all they saw were some huts and stone walls. A few local people seemed to be living there. They offered Hiram water and cooked sweet potatoes.

The view from this spot was magnificent. Hiram could see down to the river valley far below. He could also see up to the snowy mountains high overhead. It was like living in the clouds.

But had he come all this way for nothing more than an incredible view of nature?

No. As soon as he walked a little farther and rounded a corner, he came upon something incredible. There was an entire city of ruins.

Hiram had not found Vilcabamba. Instead, he had found something much better—the hidden city of Machu Picchu (say: MAT-choo PEE-choo). It was an Inca city that no one in the outside world even knew existed.

SOUTH AMERICA, 1911

CHAPTER 1
Who Were the Incas?

Many hundreds of years ago, long before the time of European explorers, native peoples lived in tribes in both North and South America.

They hunted, fished, grew crops, and sometimes fought. Their lives were simple.

But in the 1400s, in one area of South America, a tribe called the Incas did much more than that. The king ruled over a vast empire. Its capital was a city called Cuzco. There were roads and stone houses. The Incas created wonderful art. They learned how to work with metals like copper and bronze, and to make gold and silver jewelry. They wove special fabrics with fancy designs for the royalty. They studied the sky to learn about the sun, moon, and stars.

Although they didn't have written language, the Incas kept records of everything. They used a system of knots tied on strings. These were called quipus (say: KEE-poos). With the quipus, they could keep track of how much land they owned. They also kept count of how many people lived in the Inca world.

Where Is Cuzco?

Cuzco is located high in the Andes mountains of Peru. It is over eleven thousand feet—more than two miles—above sea level. Even so, the mountaintops still tower above it. Cuzco was the right place for the Inca capital city because the land was flat with mountains on all sides. The mountains protected the capital from invaders. Enemy armies would have to cross rugged terrain to reach the city. Cuzco is about seven hundred miles from Lima, the present-day capital of Peru. Today, about 350,000 people live in Cuzco.

The Incas believed that they were a special people, chosen by their gods. They worshipped the sun, and built stone temples for religious ceremonies. The temple in Cuzco was an incredible building, decorated with real gold. It was made out of stones cut so perfectly that they fitted tightly together, without cement or mortar.

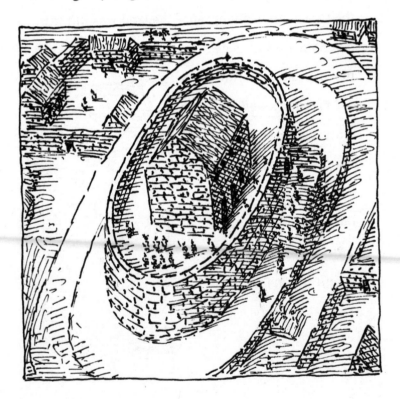

Inside the temple was a golden statue of the sun god, named Inti. He was shown as a boy, with snakes and lions coming out of his body.

Outside, there were life-size animal statues made of gold—monkeys, llamas, guinea pigs, jaguars, birds, and butterflies. All gold!

There was even a garden filled with life-size golden corn plants.

There were also niches inside the temples. Niches are indented spaces in a wall that usually hold a statue. But the Incas didn't put statues in niches. On special occasions, they put mummies in them instead!

Whenever an Inca king died, his body was mummified. It was treated in a way that would stop it from rotting. The mummy was cared for as if it were still alive. People offered food to the mummy. They presented gifts to the mummy and dressed it in the best clothing, with gold and feathers. The mummy could then be carried around, from place to place, wherever the new king went. Servants were always nearby to keep flies away from the mummy. During ceremonies and rituals, the mummies were placed in the temple niches, a place of honor.

The Incas hadn't always been a strong nation. In the early 1400s, the tribe was small and weak. But their city of Cuzco had great weather and good soil for growing crops. It made living there easy. A rival tribe called the Chancas wanted to live there, too. So the Chancas began marching toward Cuzco, planning to attack.

The Inca king was old and afraid. He ran away and hid. But his son was smart and strong. He quickly made friends with other small tribes and put together an army. They marched out to fight the Chancas before the Chancas could attack them.

The Incas fought a bloody battle with spiked wooden clubs. They won by capturing the mummy

of the Chanca king. The Chancas thought they had no power without their mummy king. So they gave up. Then the Inca king's son became the new king.

The young king chose a new name for himself—Pachacuti (say: patch-a-KOO-tee). It meant "earth-shaker" or "someone who turns the world upside down." The new king had just done that—he had turned the world upside down by defeating the Chancas.

Pretty soon, he would shake—and shape—the Inca world even more.

Quechua: Language of the Incas

The ancient Inca people spoke a language called Quechua (say: KET-chew-ah). It is still spoken today by millions of people living in Peru and other parts of South America. In the Quechua language, the word Inca meant "king." Over the years, though, outsiders began to use the word Inca to mean all the people who were part of that ancient society.

KING PACHACUTI

CHAPTER 2
Palaces and More Palaces

Little by little, Pachacuti changed the Inca world. First, he rebuilt Cuzco. He turned it into the glorious golden city that he thought it should be. The old temple had not been made with finely cut stones or golden objects. Pachacuti replaced it with a spectacular new temple to the sun. Even the walls of the temple were covered in gold. He also ordered more buildings to be created for his new government.

Then Pachacuti expanded the Inca empire. He decided the best way to protect his people and land was to make sure the neighbors wouldn't attack. How was he going to do that?

He attacked them first.

Pachacuti wore a puma skin on his head

whenever he went into battle. Each time he defeated a tribe, he put the conquered peasants to work in his army. The peasants built roads as they marched along. They also planted fields and grew huge crops of food. Soon the Inca empire spread in every direction.

Some tribes fought back against the Incas. Pachacuti defeated them. But other tribes agreed peacefully to become part of the Inca empire. Why? Pachacuti was smart. He offered gifts to rival leaders. He promised to make them rich and let their family members become royalty. He also promised to keep all the native people well fed. He held huge feasts for them, with meats, corn beer, and potatoes.

SOUTH AMERICA

In exchange, though, the peasants had to pay taxes to the king. That was on top of all the hard work they were already doing, building roads and palaces. Pachacuti got richer and richer this way.

By the 1500s, the Incas controlled almost half a million square miles of land along the western coast of South America. Their territory spread into parts of what today are six countries: Peru, Bolivia, Ecuador, Colombia, Chile, and Argentina. It was the largest empire ever to exist in South America.

Each time Pachacuti defeated a big tribe, he celebrated by building a palace and an estate on their land. An estate is a large group of houses for family, friends, and servants to live in. When he defeated a tribe called the Cuyos, Pachacuti built a palace called Pisac. It had gardens, a temple, fountains, baths, and housing for the royal family. It was a great place to come for a rest or vacation, when Pachacuti wanted to leave Cuzco.

Pachacuti attacked and conquered the Tambos. To celebrate, he built a palace and estate called Ollantaytambo (say: oy-YAN-tie-TAM-bo).

OLLANTAYTAMBO

Both palaces were in wide-open valleys. They weren't hidden from view the way Machu Picchu would become centuries later. So they were never "lost." People never stopped living in Pisac and Ollantaytambo. In fact, the two cities still exist today.

But in the 1450s, Pachacuti conquered the tribes that lived in the valley north of Cuzco. Then he built the best palace of all. It was hidden high up in the mountains, far from view. It was the palace that Hiram Bingham found in 1911—the palace now called Machu Picchu.

What Does Machu Picchu Mean?

In the language of the Incas, Machu means "old" and Picchu means "peak" or mountain. So Machu Picchu was named after the mountain on which Pachacuti had built his most beautiful palace. It was surrounded by other mountains, including an incredible peak—a tall cone-shaped mountain called Huayna Picchu. Huayna means "young." Huayna Picchu was the "young peak." Although the ruins of Machu Picchu are named after the mountain, it is not known if the Inca kings had a different name for the settlement in the past.

HUAYNA PICCHU

CHAPTER 3
The Palace at Machu Picchu

It's easy to see why Pachacuti would want a winter palace high up in the mountains. It was a perfect place to get away from the crowds in Cuzco, for one thing. It was also one of the most amazing spots for miles around. Filmy clouds draped the nearby mountains like scarves around a woman's neck. From this perch in the sky, Pachacuti could see the sun, which he worshipped. He and his priests could also track the movement of stars in the sky.

And Machu Picchu was a safe place for

a king to be with his family and friends. From the valley, looking up, no one could see the small city. If enemies attacked the Incas, they probably wouldn't even know where the Inca king was living.

Machu Picchu was a long way from Cuzco—several days' journey. Everything needed for life at the palace would have to be right there. So Pachacuti would need to build lots of houses for several hundred servants to live in. He would also need a place to plant crops to provide enough food for everyone. A steep mountainside wasn't the best place to plant fields of corn or potatoes. What to do?

The Incas were very good at engineering—at figuring out how to build things and make them work. So Pachacuti ordered his staff to create a series of terraces on which crops could be planted. Terraces are large flat areas that go down a hillside like giant steps.

First the Inca workers had to dig out soil from the steep mountain slope. They had to remove enough of the rocky dirt to create a flat area. Then they filled in the newly flattened space with layers of stones, gravel, and sand. Why? With a solid base under their plantings, the whole thing wouldn't wash away in the rain or be destroyed during an earthquake. Finally, they hauled rich soil up from the valley to the terrace.

A few feet lower—just a little way down the mountain from that terrace—they built another terrace. And another. Each terrace became a field for crops. Maize (another name for corn), potatoes, and beans were all grown at Machu Picchu.

The houses and temples Pachucuti built were made of the finest white stone. The stones were found right there on the mountain. Workers may have dug some of them out of the ground, or they may have just used huge boulders that had already broken free. They cut and shaped them without metal tools of any kind, using rocks as hammers to chip away at the stone.

Pachacuti is said to have measured out the size for each building himself, with string. For the royal houses, the large stones were perfectly cut and fitted together. Some of the stones weighed as much as fourteen tons! Moving them was incredibly hard work, since the Incas didn't have wheels or carts.

For the servants' houses, the stones weren't as smoothly or carefully cut, but they were still strong. All the buildings were covered with thatched roofs made out of a kind of long grass.

The royal houses were on the highest part of the estate, looking down. Peasants and workers lived below. Pachacuti's own house was at the top, with a wall all around it for privacy. His house was large but not huge—a bit smaller than a modern basketball court. It wasn't fancy like a palace. But it was well protected, with two gates made out of enormous stones, to keep his enemies out.

The king's house had another special feature, too—a private bathroom. It was the only house at Machu Picchu with running water in it.

Getting water to the palace at Machu Picchu was tricky because of the mountain location. The only source of water was a spring high up on the slope. So the Inca engineers built aqueducts.

Aqueducts are stone troughs or channels that carry water a long distance, to where people live. At Machu Picchu, the aqueduct brought very pure water from half a mile away. It flowed down the aqueduct and into sixteen different stone fountains. Then it shot out like a jet. Since Pachacuti lived at the top of the estate, the water flowed to him first. No one had touched the water before it reached him, so it was at its purest.

More than a hundred members of the royal family could stay at Machu Picchu—with as many as five hundred servants. Outside the estate there were smaller houses for people who had been conquered by Pachacuti. They were probably slaves.

What was life like at Machu Picchu? For the king, a man who loved nature, each day was spent enjoying the beauty of the world around him. For his many servants, it was a life of hard work carried out in a very beautiful place.

CHAPTER 4
Life in the Clouds

The buildings at Machu Picchu are in ruins now. The roofs are gone. So are most of the personal items the king would have used while he was alive. But scientists can still figure out how Pachacuti lived and what he thought was important. How? By looking at the way he chose to build his most beautiful private retreat.

The most important thing in Pachacuti's life—at least while he was at his winter palace—was his respect for nature. So all of the religious buildings at Machu Picchu were designed to include parts of nature in their structure. Sometimes a temple was built right into the side of the mountain. Or a gigantic natural rock would become an altar, with cut stones added to the base.

TEMPLE OF THE MOON

The temples were also designed so the Incas would have views of the constellations from their windows. Astronomers—people who study the stars and planets—helped figure out where the windows should go. Each day, the priests at

Machu Picchu would perform ceremonies to honor the sun and moon gods.

The main temple is thought to have been designed so that one window lined up with a view of a cluster of stars called the Pleiades in the morning sky. Another window was positioned so that on the shortest day of the year (which was in late June), the sun would shine through onto an altar in the center of the floor. That day is called the winter solstice. Special ceremonies were held on the winter solstice in Pachacuti's time, and the solstice is still celebrated today.

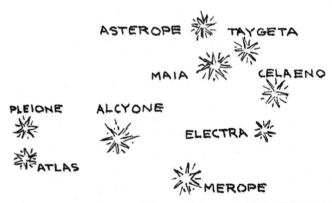

THE PLEIADES STAR CLUSTER

Winter and Summer in South America

Because the earth travels around the sun on a tilted axis, the top half and bottom half of the globe have winter and summer at opposite times of the year. Most of South America, including Machu Picchu, is in the bottom half of the globe. The colder weather of winter arrives during the months of June, July, and August. Summer comes in December, January, and February.

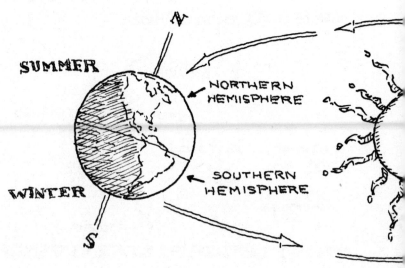

When it's summer in Machu Picchu, it's winter in New York City, and vice versa. But even in winter, the weather in Peru is pretty mild. The average temperature in Machu Picchu is about sixty-five degrees Fahrenheit. It stays sunny, dry, and cool. It never snows in Peru except on the mountaintops.

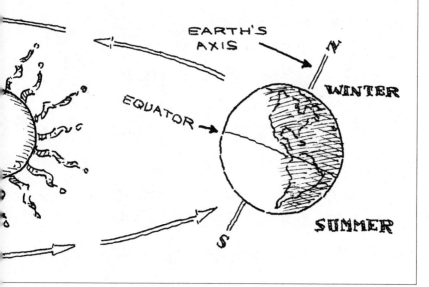

Rainbows often appeared in the sky at Machu Picchu, and they still do today. The Incas believed that rainbows had magical power. They helped the Inca king talk to the sun god. So the main temple at Machu Picchu was built in the shape of a rainbow, with a curved wall. Some warriors also had pictures of rainbows on their shields.

Pachacuti loved flowers and sang songs about them. People say he sang a song about the lilies as he was dying. Today, more than ninety kinds of orchids from Pachacuti's time have been found still growing at Machu Picchu.

The king spent much of his time outdoors hunting. He and his guests captured alpacas and llamas, which lived even higher up in the mountains. They hunted smaller animals and deer. The meat from hunted animals was eaten at feasts and celebrations for the workers. Llamas and alpacas were usually kept as herd animals, but were also eaten as meat. The wool from the alpacas was woven into the softest clothing, worn only by the royal family. Sometimes they used an animal as part of a ritual sacrifice. They killed the animal and then offered it to the sun god.

Llamas and Alpacas

Llamas are smart, gentle woolly animals that live in herds. They are related to camels and are used as pack animals—to carry heavy loads. Llamas can be trained easily, but if they don't like something, they'll spit at it! Their green spit comes up from the contents of their stomachs. It can fly up to ten feet away.

Llamas weigh about four hundred pounds. They're six feet tall at the tops of their heads. Alpacas are softer, woollier, and smaller. Their fine wool comes in dozens of different colors. Alpacas are in the camel family, too—which means they're in the spitting family. Watch out!

ALPACA   LLAMA

There were enough servants at Machu Picchu to provide anything the king might want. Some wove textiles from the alpaca wool. Others made gold and silver jewelry. The gold came from a mine in Peru; even today Peru has one of the world's largest gold mines. Shawl pins made of bronze or silver were also popular. They were long tapered metal pins used to hold a shawl closed, since the Incas didn't have buttons.

SHAWL PIN

Pachacuti probably spent the winter months, from May through September, at Machu Picchu. Then it was time to make the long journey down the road, back to Cuzco. The Inca kings needed to spend much of the year in the capital city to run the government. They had to be there in case anyone tried to take over their empire.

In 1532, Spanish invaders did just that.

CHAPTER 5
Invaders!

For almost one hundred years, from 1438 to the 1530s, the Inca empire was strong. Incas ruled a huge area in South America. Until the late 1400s, no one in Europe even knew that North and South America existed. But Christopher Columbus's voyages, beginning in 1492, changed that. His

CHRISTOPHER
COLUMBUS

discoveries set off a feverish age of exploration. Other explorers wanted to follow in Columbus's footsteps. They wanted to find lands to conquer—especially if there was gold.

The Spanish explorers and invaders who arrived

in South America were called *conquistadors* (say: kon-KEES-ta-DORS).

One conquistador was a man named Francisco Pizarro. He reached Panama by ship with a small group of soldiers and horses in 1513, and later became mayor of the newly founded Panama City. Pizarro had heard that there was a lot of gold, but he had no idea how much. When he saw all the gold the Incas possessed, he decided right then and there to conquer this land. He stood on the beach where he had landed and claimed it for Spain.

FRANCISCO PIZARRO

The Age of Discovery

The period of time from the late 1400s to the 1600s is called the Age of Discovery or the Age of Exploration. During that time, Europeans sailed around the world. They were looking for lands or new peoples to trade with. Many countries, especially England and Spain, competed with each other. They wanted these new lands, which belonged to native peoples, for themselves. In many cases, the explorers conquered the native people and took over their land. The early explorers thought they had discovered a whole New World. But the "New World" they found had been there all along. They didn't discover it—the people living there already knew about it! So the word *discovery* was wrong in many ways.

By the time Pizarro arrived, Pachacuti was long dead. A new Inca king was in charge. His name was Atahuallpa (say: ah-ta-HUAL-pa). He had just become ruler of the Incas after defeating his own brother in a long battle, which weakened the Incas.

Atahuallpa had an army of thousands—maybe as many as eighty thousand soldiers. So he figured he could defeat the Spanish invaders. After all, there were fewer than two hundred of Pizarro's men. The Inca king agreed to meet Pizarro in the center of Cajamarca, a city north of Cuzco.

Atahuallpa was confident of his power and left most of his army outside the city. The soldiers who came in with him—about five thousand—were unarmed.

That was a big mistake.

Pizarro and his men had two things the Incas didn't have—horses and guns. When Atahuallpa was carried into the city on his throne, the Spanish were hiding. They sprang out and fired their guns at the Incas. They killed many of the guards and took Atahuallpa captive.

Francisco Pizarro (c. 1475–1541)

Pizarro was a hard-hearted, brave, brutal, ambitious man from a poor part of Spain. He didn't know how to read or write, but he was desperate to make a fortune as an explorer. He sailed from Spain to Panama, where he was granted land and slaves by the governor. There he heard stories of an incredible kingdom of gold. He sailed south to Peru, where the gold was rumored to be.

Pizarro had agreed to share any treasure with his men. But partway through the trip, Pizarro's men became sick and wanted to go home. Pizarro stood on the beach and drew a line in the sand. The line, he said, stood for the difference between being safe and being rich. Men who crossed the line might face hunger, thirst, and sickness—but they could also be rewarded with tremendous wealth. Pizarro dared his men to cross the line and come with him. The thirteen who did became rich beyond their wildest dreams.

Atahuallpa tried to bargain with Pizarro. He offered to fill a huge room with gold and silver, as a gift to the Spanish invader. A whole room full of gold? Pizarro was amazed. Atahuallpa said it would take a year to bring all the gold to Pizarro, since most of it was in Cuzco, hundreds of miles away.

For the next several months, the Incas brought gold and silver objects to Pizarro—six hundred pounds each day! Gold plates and cups, jewelry, pitchers, jars full of emeralds, and statues from the temple were delivered. Pizarro had agreed to the deal, but he probably never meant to keep

his word. While he was waiting for the gold, he played chess with Atahuallpa and treated him well. A few months later, though, Pizarro killed the Inca king.

According to legend, when the Incas heard the king had been killed, they hid the rest of the gold. Tons of golden objects were hidden in a mountain cave for many years. Treasure hunters have searched for it, but no one knows for sure whether it was ever found, or even if it ever existed. Some people think the secret fortune in gold may still be hidden there today.

The Spanish melted down most of the beautiful golden objects they'd received, including the life-size garden of golden corn. They used it to make ingots (metal bars) and coins. Some of the treasure was sent back to the king of Spain. Only one piece of gold corn survives today, in a museum.

After that, the Spanish ruled the Incas by putting "puppet kings" in power. The puppet kings didn't act on their own. They did whatever the Spanish told them to do. These rulers weren't really in charge of their own country. But one king, named Manco Inca, tried to rebel against the Spanish. He fled to the city of Vilcabamba

MANCO INCA

and tried to fight the Spanish off for the next eight years, until he was killed.

The Incas continued the fight, but eventually lost. By 1572, their empire was gone and their whole way of life was being rubbed out by the Spanish. Over time, the city of Vilcabamba disappeared—and became covered by the jungle that surrounded it.

As for the magnificent palace at Machu Picchu, it had been lost from sight for decades. Once an Inca king died, the next Inca king was not allowed to use the previous king's palaces. So within a few decades of Pachacuti's death, the jungle vines and forest grew over the buildings at Machu Picchu and covered them.

By the time the Spanish arrived, the palace was already hidden. The Spanish probably never even knew it was there. Only a handful of people would see it from that time on—until Hiram Bingham arrived four hundred years later.

CHAPTER 6
Who Was Hiram Bingham III?

Ever since he was a boy, Hiram Bingham III had longed for adventure.

Growing up in Hawaii, the son of a very strict preacher, Hiram's life at home had been filled with rules. Whenever Hiram broke the rules, his father hit him with a stick. His parents read the Bible all the time. They didn't believe in dancing or having fun. Hiram's only joy was reading. He especially loved Mark Twain's *The Adventures of Huckleberry Finn*. Later in life, he loved stories and poems by Rudyard Kipling. His favorite poem was called "The Explorer." One of the lines in the poem said: "Something hidden. Go and find it." Hiram Bingham III had dreamed of doing just that.

When Hiram was twelve years old, he decided
to run away from home. He didn't want to just
wander down the street for a few hours. He made
an elaborate plan to travel thousands of miles to
New York—and then to Africa! He packed a bag
and left the house, as if he were going to school.

Then he went to the bank, where he took out all the money he had saved for college—$250. He and a friend bought tickets on a ship that was leaving that day. It was going to San Francisco, on the west coast of the United States. Hiram planned to get to New York City on his own somehow. He thought he could earn money as a newsboy. When he had enough saved, he would sail for England and eventually go exploring in Africa.

Rudyard Kipling (1865–1936)

Rudyard Kipling was a British writer who was born in India. When he was six years old, he was sent to live with an unpleasant family in England. At sixteen, he went back to live in India and worked for a newspaper. Eventually he sailed all over the world and landed in America. He met the famous American writer Mark Twain, and then moved to Vermont. He wrote *The Jungle Book* along with many poems  and novels. In 1896, he moved back to England, but he never stopped exploring. He sailed to Africa, just as Hiram Bingham hoped to do. In 1907, Kipling won the Nobel Prize for Literature—the highest honor a writer can receive.

But the ship that was supposed to leave that day was delayed—and Hiram's friend chickened out. The friend went home and told his own father about the plan. Soon Hiram's father showed up on the dock. He put an end to the whole thing. Hiram would have to wait a few more years for his life of adventure to begin.

Still, after that, his father let him have more freedom. And a few years later, when he was sixteen, Hiram was sent to boarding school in Massachusetts. After boarding school, he went on to study at Yale University and Harvard University. Eventually, he became a professor of South American history at Yale.

YALE UNIVERSITY

In 1900, he married Alfreda Mitchell, the granddaughter of Charles L. Tiffany—the man

ALFREDA MITCHELL

who started the famous jewelry store in New York. They had seven sons.

But the stuffy, quiet life of a professor was not what Hiram had hoped for. In December 1908, he got the chance to travel to South America for a meeting of professors and scientists. He jumped at the opportunity.

After the meeting, which was held in Chile, Hiram went on to Cuzco in Peru. There he met a man from the government. His name was Juan Nuñez (say: NOON-yez). Nuñez told him about some ancient ruins. Hiram wasn't an archaeologist—a scientist who studies ancient peoples by digging up their buildings and finding things they used long ago. He was a history professor. But Nuñez insisted that he come along to see the ruins Nuñez had visited.

Those first ruins were interesting—but not exciting. Hiram knew they couldn't possibly be the lost city of Vilcabamba, the home of the last rulers of the Incas. That was what he longed to find.

Still, Hiram had brought along a camera, so he took some pictures. He also had with him a book called *Hints to Travellers*. The book said that if a traveler found some ruins, he should make careful measurements of the site. It also said he should write down complete descriptions of everything he saw.

Hiram did all of that. He even made a map of the site. He would need all these things to show other professors and experts when he got back home.

Whether he knew it or not right then, Hiram was going to come back to South America to search for Vilcabamba. He was now setting forth on a life of adventure just as he had always wanted. If he found Vilcabamba, the discovery would put his own name in the history books. For a history professor, that would be a very big deal.

Hiram Bingham and Indiana Jones

Was Indiana Jones based on Hiram Bingham? It's very possible. The first movie begins with Indiana Jones running through a jungle in Peru, carrying a bullwhip and looking for lost treasure. But in the next scene, he's back at his job as a mild-mannered college professor—just like Hiram Bingham. When *Raiders of the Lost Ark* came out in 1981, audiences laughed at the surprising idea that an action hero could also

 be a quiet professor. Hiram Bingham wasn't exactly an action hero, but his search for a lost Inca city was probably one inspiration for the Indiana Jones movies.

CHAPTER 7
The Discovery

Within two years of returning to the United States, Hiram was ready to leave again.

His wife didn't want him to go. It wasn't a good time. She had just had a baby, and her father had just died. But nothing was going to stop Hiram Bingham from exploring. In fact, in 1910, his name was included in a book called *Who's Who in America*—a list of famous people. Hiram had the publishers list his job as "Explorer," even though at the time he was mainly a history professor at Yale.

Before he could leave for South America, Hiram had to organize and plan the trip. It was called the 1911 Yale Peruvian Expedition. First, he had to find a team of experts to come along with him. Hiram chose six men—experts in subjects such as geography, chemistry, medicine, mapmaking, mountain climbing, and nature.

Then he had to raise enough money to pay for supplies and travel. It was going to cost $12,000. In 1911, that was a lot of money. It would be about a quarter of a million dollars in today's money.

Hiram sold his family's property in Hawaii to get part of the cash. He also went to *Harper's Magazine* and promised to write four articles for them when he got back. They paid Hiram in advance. Then he  asked the Kodak Company to give him cameras and film. He asked Abercrombie and Fitch, the sporting goods company, to give him a discounted price on hiking gear.

On June 8, 1911, Hiram and his team sailed from New York City to Panama and then on to Lima, Peru.

When they reached Lima, Hiram immediately began asking questions. He was like a detective trying to solve a mystery. Where should he look? He went to the library and met with a history expert. He copied down notes about Vilcabamba written by a Spanish priest in the years after Spain defeated the Incas. He went to the geographical society—a place where old as well as new maps were kept. He bought several maps that might help. He also met with the president of Peru. The president sent three army sergeants along with Hiram's group, to make sure they would be safe.

Next, Hiram and his team took a train to Cuzco. When he got there, he asked more questions about the lost city he was searching for. Several local people knew—or suspected—that there were some wonderful ruins north of Cuzco.

Rumors of the ruins at Machu Picchu had probably come from peasants who lived nearby. But no one from the city of Cuzco or anywhere else had bothered to go check them out.

Hiram met a fellow American who was a professor at the University of Cuzco. His name was Albert Giesecke. He gave Hiram Bingham the best clue of all. He told Hiram how to find a man named Melchor Arteaga. A while back, in January, Melchor had offered to show Giesecke some fabulous ruins. But it had been the rainy season then—a bad time for climbing a slippery mountain—so Giesecke didn't go.

Hiram decided to divide the scientists in his group into three teams. Two of the teams were sent off on their own, to make maps of the valleys and towns nearby. Hiram's group was to search for Inca ruins. They would also collect insects. One of the members of Hiram's team was a specialist who collected nature samples.

It took five days for Hiram's small group to travel by mule to the river valley where Melchor lived. On the way, Hiram's team visited the ruins of another one of Pachacuti's royal palaces—the palace at Ollantaytambo. Then they pitched some tents near the grass-thatched hut where Melchor lived.

On the sixth day, Hiram was ready to see the ruins that Melchor had described. He dressed for the trip, wearing tall boots, khaki pants, a jacket with many pockets, a scarf at his neck, and a brimmed hat. The lower part of his legs were tightly wrapped in strips of heavy cloth to protect him from snake bites.

But it was cold and drizzly that morning. Melchor didn't seem to want to go. Hiram offered him a Peruvian silver dollar—three or four times as much money as a guide would normally charge. Finally, Melchor agreed to lead Hiram and a sergeant up the mountain to Machu Picchu. The others stayed behind.

At the top of the mountain, there were indeed ruins. In fact, three families of peasant farmers had been living there for four years. They had cleared some of the terraces from the forgotten royal palace and were growing crops. They offered Hiram and the other two men water from a gourd—a kind of cup made from a hollowed-out fruit. They also gave them cooked sweet potatoes to eat while they rested.

Then Melchor sat and chatted with the family while Hiram and the sergeant went to explore the ruins. At first, he didn't think there was much to see. But the family sent a young boy along with him, to show him the way. The boy led them,

climbing through thick shrubs and vines growing over the terraces. Then they climbed up and over the terrace walls, and farther up a steep hill with some stone steps. Much of it was overgrown. At first, it was hard to see much.

But eventually they came to what Hiram had been hoping for—fabulous ancient buildings made of perfectly cut blocks of white stone. He thought that two of the buildings had the finest stonework he'd ever seen. Each time he rounded a corner or climbed to another terrace, he found something more—another temple, another group of houses.

For the next five hours, Hiram explored the ruins and took pictures of them. In many of the pictures, he had the boy or the sergeant pose as well. It was the best way to show how big the buildings actually were. Hiram made careful notes, too, so he could write about this discovery when he got back home.

Of course, Hiram wasn't the first person ever to see the abandoned ruins at Machu Picchu. Other peasants, besides the ones living in the ruins, knew about the place. Hiram also found a man's name written on one of the temple walls.

It said *Lizarraga*, with the date 1902. Agustin Lizarraga was a local farmer who had explored the site years before Hiram got there.

But Hiram Bingham's visit that day in 1911 would be remembered in history books forever. It was the first time Machu Picchu was known to the outside world—and it would turn out to be one of the most incredible sites in all of South America.

CHAPTER 8
Mistakes

Hiram Bingham made a number of mistakes after he found Machu Picchu.

His first mistake was leaving right after he found it. He was excited when he saw the ruins at Machu Picchu—but he was disappointed at the same time. He desperately wanted to find the lost city of Vilcabamba. Hiram thought finding Vilcabamba was the best way to become famous.

So, after he photographed Machu Picchu for one day, he moved on.

He spent the next few weeks searching for the city where the Inca empire had died out. He *almost* found it—but he didn't realize it. The ruins he stumbled onto were so overgrown with jungle, he couldn't see what was there. And the buildings were much less beautiful than those at Machu Picchu. So Hiram figured this couldn't possibly be the famous city that he was seeking.

Hiram finally gave up and went home. He had found Vilcabamba without knowing it! The lost city wasn't correctly identified until more than fifty years later, by another explorer who came to Peru in 1964. Hiram had been right about one thing, though. The ruins at Vilcabamba were nothing compared to the gorgeous mountaintop palace he had found.

By this time, one of Hiram's dreams had come true. He was famous. His discovery of Machu Picchu was more than enough to excite the world. Hiram wrote articles about it. Then he organized another expedition back to Peru in 1912. This time, he took more scientists with him. He also hired a team of workers to uncover more of the buildings that were overgrown with moss and vines.

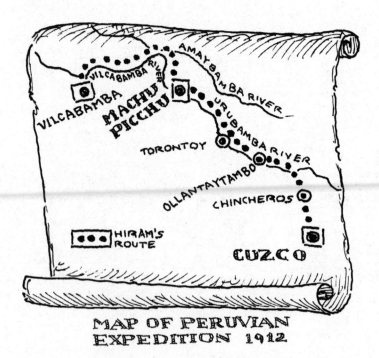

MAP OF PERUVIAN
EXPEDITION 1912

Hiram's team dug in the ground at Machu Picchu and found jewelry, pots, and tools. They also found burial caves. But the caves contained only small skeletons. Most of them were less than five feet tall. So Hiram made another mistake. He decided that all the skeletons must be women! He came up with an idea to explain why only women were living at Machu Picchu. He said the city had been a special place for female priestesses—like nuns. He called them the Virgins of the Sun.

Hiram was wrong about the skeletons. It turns out that the ancient Incas were short—the men as well as the women. Even today, most of the people who speak Quechua are shorter than people in the United States. The men are about five feet two inches tall and the women are several inches shorter. So the small skeletons Hiram had found were both men and women.

After his second trip, Hiram wrote more about Machu Picchu. *National Geographic* magazine printed a whole issue on just that one topic.

His photographs amazed everyone. But many of Hiram's facts were wrong. He claimed that Machu Picchu must have been the *first* Inca capital. He was wrong about that. But Hiram wasn't a scientist. He was a history professor, just doing his best to figure out what the ruins could tell him about ancient Inca life.

Hiram did something else that would be considered wrong today. He took thousands of objects from Machu Picchu. With the permission of the government of Peru, he brought jewelry, carvings, tools, and skeletons back to the United States. He donated them to Yale University. For years, the Peabody Museum at Yale had a large exhibit of Inca items on display.

But today, explorers are not allowed to remove ancient items from a country, because each country has a right to keep the historical objects that are clues to its own past. So Peru asked Yale to return the Inca treasures. In 2011—one hundred years after Hiram's discovery—the Peabody Museum finally agreed.

Still, Hiram is considered a hero, even in Peru. In 1948, Peru built a new road leading up to the ruins. They named it for him—the Hiram Bingham Highway.

Now, thanks to that road, visitors can make the trip up the mountain to Machu Picchu a lot more easily than when Hiram crawled there on his hands and knees!

CHAPTER 9
Visit to a Lost City

The road that Hiram took to Machu Picchu is called the Inca Trail. It still exists today. The path winds up and down hills for many miles. It passes through cloud forests and beside lakes. Deer are seen along the way, and orchids bloom. It is a natural wonderland filled with birds and butterflies. More than three hundred kinds of butterflies are seen in the daytime. Another four hundred kinds come out at night!

SYLPHINA ANGEL DAINTY EGG WHITE

Sometimes rare endangered animals will wander into sight. In 2001, a spectacled bear walked right into Machu Picchu! (Spectacled bears have markings on their faces that make it look like they're wearing eyeglasses.) Then it ambled down some steps and back into the forest.

Llamas and alpacas still live on the mountain and roam freely among the ruins.

The Inca Trail itself is beautiful, too. It is covered with stones that the Incas cut and laid themselves. One part of the trail includes a climb up approximately 1,500 steps made by the Incas. In the days of Pachacuti, the trail was a private road, used only by royalty.

These days, two thousand people visit Machu Picchu every single day. A small number—a couple hundred each day—arrive just like Hiram Bingham did. They hike along the Inca Trail for four or five days. Porters carry tents, and guides lead the way. Then the visitors climb more than a thousand steps to the ruins at the top. There they pass through a gate that was the original entrance to Machu Picchu.

Most people, though, arrive from Cuzco by train. They take a bus up the steep mountain to the ruins.

There is a charge to enter Machu Picchu—it's now a national park. There is a bathroom and a snack bar outside the ruins. Otherwise, the country of Peru has tried as much as possible to preserve the site as it was four hundred years ago.

In recent years, there was talk of building a cable car to carry tourists up to the palace. Most people in Peru were strongly against it. They felt it would spoil the natural beauty of the spot. Candidates running for president of Peru in 2001 debated about it on TV. But Machu Picchu is a World Heritage Site—a place that should never be destroyed or changed. (Other World Heritage Sites include the Great Pyramids, the Grand Canyon, and the Statue of Liberty.) Most people in Peru hope that the cable car will never be built.

Scientists still come to study Machu Picchu. In the 1990s, scientists cleared out two of the aqueducts and fountains that Pachacuti had built. As soon as they removed all the dirt blocking the stone channels, water burst out of the spout! Today, all sixteen fountains carry water, but most of the water is provided by hidden hoses.

The Incas may be gone, but important parts of their culture still live on. The Quechua language is still alive. It is spoken by as many as fourteen million native people, mainly in the Andes mountains. Native people still celebrate some of the Inca traditions, too. They worship the mountains and make offerings of corn beer to the spirit gods.

In Cuzco, Peruvian people celebrate the winter solstice every year in June during the Festival of the Sun. The festival involves music, parades, and dancing. They also hold feasts and celebrations in August, to give thanks for the growing season.

Sometimes the people prepare food packages as an offering to the gods. The food is carried to Inca ruins nearby and burned on huge bonfires after midnight. They believe that the spirit gods will inhale the smoke.

Machu Picchu is probably the most treasured site in Peru—and maybe in all of South America. Other countries sometimes advertise trips and tours to Machu Picchu—even though it isn't located in their country! They hope tourists will visit their country thinking Machu Picchu is nearby.

But the people of Peru hope Machu Picchu will not have *too many* visitors. To prevent damage, the government limits the number of people who can walk on those ancient stone paths every day. Now that this magnificent lost city is famous the world over, it's more important than ever to protect it, and to show respect for the things the Incas valued—the beauty of nature and the artistry that human beings can achieve.

Timeline of Machu Picchu

1438	Pachacuti becomes king of the Incas
1450–1470	Machu Picchu built
1471	Pachacuti dies. His son, Tupac Inca, becomes king
1492	Columbus sails west to new lands and sets off the Age of Discovery
1532	Pizarro imprisons Atahuallpa in the town of Cajamarca
1537	Manco Inca rebels against the Spanish and goes to Vilcabamba, the new capital city
1572	Spanish defeat the last Incas at Vilcabamba
1875	Hiram Bingham III born
1888	Hiram tries to run away from home
1911	Hiram discovers ruins of Machu Picchu
1912	Second Yale Peruvian Expedition
1913	First articles and photos of Machu Picchu published in *Harper's Magazine* and *National Geographic*
1948	Road leading to Machu Picchu is named for Bingham
2011	Yale's Peabody Museum begins to return Inca treasures to Peru

Timeline of the World

1440 — Johannes Gutenberg invents modern movable type printing in Europe

1488 — Bartolomeu Dias sails around the southernmost tip of Africa

1522 — Ferdinand Magellan's crew completes the first circumnavigation of the world

1533 — Queen Elizabeth I is born

1542 — Spanish explorers begin to map the California coast

1588 — Britain defeats the Spanish Armada

1637 — Pedro Teixeira explores the full length of the Amazon River

1873 — Jules Verne publishes *Around the World in Eighty Days*

1879 — Thomas Alva Edison invents workable electric light

1885 — The Home Insurance Building, considered the world's first skyscraper, is built in Chicago

1892 — Ellis Island is opened for immigrant inspection

1896 — First modern Olympic Games are held in Athens, Greece

1909 — American explorers Peary and Henson reach the North Pole

1912 — The "unsinkable" *Titanic* strikes an iceberg and sinks into the North Atlantic

1937 — American pilot Amelia Earhart disappears somewhere in the Pacific

1945 — End of World War II

2012 — Superstorm Sandy strikes the northeast United States

Bibliography

*Books for young readers

Adams, Mark. *Turn Right at Machu Picchu*. New York: Plume, 2011.

Burger, Richard L., and Lucy C. Salazar. *Machu Picchu: Unveiling the Mystery of the Incas*. New Haven: Yale University Press, 2004.

Dudenhoefer, David, et. al. *Fodor's Peru*. 6th edition. New York: Random House, 2015.

*Lewin, Ted. *Lost City: The Discovery of Machu Picchu*. New York: Puffin Books, 2003.

MacQuarrie, Kim. *The Last Days of the Incas*. New York: Simon & Schuster, 2007.

Protzen, Jean-Pierre. "Inca Quarrying and Stone Cutting." Chicago: *Journal of the Society of Architectural Historians*, Vol. 44, No. 2; May 1985.